HISTORY'S MOST INFLUENTIAL

PHILOSOPHERS

FROM THE Mid-1900s TO THE Present

Hannah Arendt to Peter Singer

EDITED BY BRIAN DUIGNAN

Britannica® Educational Publishing

IN ASSOCIATION WITH

ROSEN EDUCATIONAL SERVICES

Published in 2025 by Britannica Educational Publishing
(a trademark of Encyclopædia Britannica, Inc.)
in association with Rosen Educational Services, LLC
2544 Clinton Street, Buffalo, NY 14224.

Distributed exclusively by Rosen Educational Services.
For a listing of additional Britannica Educational Publishing titles, call toll free (800) 237-9932.

First Edition

Britannica Educational Publishing
Michael I. Levy: Executive Editor
Marilyn L. Barton: Senior Coordinator, Production Control
Steven Bosco: Director, Editorial Technologies
Lisa S. Braucher: Senior Producer and Data Editor
Yvette Charboneau: Senior Copy Editor
Kathy Nakamura: Manager, Media Acquisition
Robert Curley: Manager, Science and Technology

Editor: Greg Roza
Book design: Michael Flynn

Photo credits: Cover, p. 30 4.murat/Shutterstock.com; p. 7 https://commons.wikimedia.org/wiki/File:Hannah_Arendt_auf_dem_1._Kulturkritikerkongress,_Barbara_Niggl_Radloff,_FM-2019-1-5-9-16_(cropped).jpg; p. 34 360b/Shutterstock.com.

Cataloging-in-Publication Data

Names: Duignan, Brian.
Title: From the mid-1900s to present: Hannah Arendt to Peter Singer / edited by Brian Duignan.
Description: New York : Britannica Educational Publishing, in Association with Rosen Educational Services, 2025. | Series: History's most influential philosophers | Includes glossary and index.
Identifiers: ISBN 9781641904100 (library bound) | ISBN 9781641904094 (pbk) | ISBN 9781641904117 (ebook)
Subjects: LCSH: Philosophers--Biography. | Philosophy--History. | Philosophers--20th century--Biography.
Classification: LCC B104.F766 2025 | DDC 109.2--dc23

Manufactured in the United States of America

CPSIA Compliance Information: Batch #CWBRIT25. For further information contact Rosen Publishing at 1-800-237-9932.

CONTENTS

Introduction

"The only possible basis for a sound morality is mutual tolerance and respect: tolerance of one another's customs and opinions; respect for one another's rights and feelings; awareness of one another's needs."
—A. J. Ayer (1910–1989)

Life doesn't come with an instruction manual. Each person is left to find their own way to some sort of understanding about the mysteries of existence. As people grow and learn, they naturally ask questions. How did the world—and universe—come to exist? Why am I here? What is my purpose in life? What happens after I die?

People began their search for meaning very early on in the course of human history. Long before the age of science, they used reason to understand why things happened as they did, and to find some sort of order and security in what they saw as a chaotic and often dangerous world. They questioned, probed, and refused to accept commonly held beliefs. Through their teachings, the discipline of philosophy was born.

In the simplest terms, philosophy is about thinking. Yet philosophers do a lot more than sit around thinking and asking questions. They engage in fundamental discussions about nature, society, science, psychology, and ethics. They develop critical ideas about the way people live, and the way they should live. Traveling through the pages of this book, you will discover the events and the people that shaped philosophy from the mid-1900s to the present.

Three basic principles guide philosophical thought. The first is ontology, which is the study of existence—why we are here. Some philosophers have used philosophy to defend religion and contemplate the existence of God.

Other thinkers used philosophy to dispute religious beliefs. The British philosopher A. J. Ayer used something called the verification principle to examine religious beliefs and find that they cannot be verified as either true or false. In his view then, such religious assertions are meaningless.

The second principle of philosophy, epistemology, involves the study of knowledge—how we know what we know. This leads to ideas about the origins of knowledge and how knowledge is obtained. Many philosophers from this period also studied the related philosophy of language, including Willard Van Orman Quine, Wilfred Sellars, Richard Rorty, and David Kellogg Lewis. Noam Chomsky is a celebrated contemporary philosopher and linguist whose theories have revolutionized the understanding of language learning.

The final of the three guiding philosophical principles is ethics, or the study of what is right and wrong. The fundamental nature of humankind has long challenged the great philosophers. Are people born inherently good, evil, or somewhere in between? And how do people know which actions are good or evil, right or wrong? Peter Singer contends that the good of all sentient creatures must be considered in questions of ethics. As a utilitarian philosopher, Singer argues that the ethical duty is to choose actions that either prevent more pain than they cause or cause more happiness than they prevent.

The great thinkers whose lives and beliefs are detailed in these pages have helped give shape and depth to human existence. And yet philosophy is constantly evolving. Just as some questions are answered, new questions emerge. Expect the list of influential philosophers to grow over the years as people continue to probe and wonder about the great mysteries of the universe and human existence.

HANNAH ARENDT

(b. Oct. 14, 1906, Hannover, Ger.—d. Dec. 4, 1975, New York, N.Y., U.S.)

Hannah Arendt was a German-born American political scientist and philosopher who is known for her critical writing on Jewish affairs and her study of totalitarianism.

Arendt grew up in Hannover, Germany, and in Königsberg, Prussia (now Kaliningrad, Russia). Beginning in 1924 she studied philosophy at the Universities of Marburg, Freiburg, and Heidelberg; she received a doctoral degree in philosophy at Heidelberg in 1928. At Marburg she began a romantic relationship with her teacher, Martin Heidegger, that lasted until 1928. In 1933, when Heidegger joined the Nazi Party and began implementing Nazi educational policies as rector of Freiburg, Arendt, who was Jewish, was forced to flee to Paris. She married Heinrich Blücher, a philosophy professor, in 1940. She again became a fugitive from the Nazis in 1941, when she and her husband immigrated to the United States.

Settling in New York City, she became research director of the Conference on Jewish Relations (1944–46), chief editor of Schocken Books (1946–48), and executive director (1949–52) of Jewish Cultural Reconstruction, Inc., which sought to salvage Jewish writings dispersed by the Nazis. She was naturalized as an American citizen in 1951. She taught at the University of Chicago from 1963 to 1967 and thereafter at the New School for Social Research in New York City.

Arendt's reputation as a major political thinker was established by her *Origins of Totalitarianism* (1951), which also treated 19th-century anti-Semitism, imperialism, and racism. Arendt viewed the growth of totalitarianism

Hannah Arendt called herself a political theorist and focused her work on the nature of power, the use of authority, and the necessity of freedom.

as the outcome of the disintegration of the traditional nation-state. She argued that totalitarian regimes, through their pursuit of raw political power and their neglect of material or utilitarian considerations, had revolutionized the social structure and made contemporary politics nearly impossible to predict.

The Human Condition, published in 1958, was a wide-ranging and systematic treatment of what Arendt called the *vita activa* (Latin: "active life"). She defended the classical ideals of work, citizenship, and political action against what she considered a debased obsession with mere welfare. Like most of her work, it owed a great deal to the philosophical style of Heidegger.

In a highly controversial work, *Eichmann in Jerusalem* (1963), based on her reportage of the trial of the Nazi war criminal Adolf Eichmann in 1961, Arendt argued that Eichmann's crimes resulted not from a wicked or depraved character but from sheer "thoughtlessness": he was simply an ambitious bureaucrat who failed to reflect on the enormity of what he was doing. His role in the mass extermination of Jews epitomized "the fearsome, word-and-thought-defying banality of evil" that had spread across Europe at the time. Arendt's refusal to recognize Eichmann as "inwardly" evil prompted fierce denunciations from both Jewish and non-Jewish intellectuals.

Arendt resumed contact with Heidegger in 1950, and in subsequent essays and lectures she defended him by claiming that his Nazi involvement had been the "mistake" of a great philosopher. In the late 20th century, following the publication of a volume of letters between Arendt and Heidegger written between 1925 and 1975, some scholars suggested that Arendt's personal and intellectual attachment to her former teacher had led her to adopt a lenient assessment of him that was inconsistent with her condemnation of the collaboration of others and with her insistence in various writings that any act of compromise with evil is wholly immoral.

Arendt's other works include *Between Past and Future* (1961), *On Revolution* (1963), *Men in Dark Times* (1968), *On Violence* (1970), and *Crises of the Republic* (1972). Her unfinished manuscript *The Life of the Mind* was edited by her friend and correspondent Mary McCarthy and published in 1978. *Responsibility and Judgment*, published in 2003, collects essays and lectures on moral topics from the years following publication of *Eichmann in Jerusalem*.

SIMONE DE BEAUVOIR

(b. Jan. 9, 1908, Paris, France—d. April 14, 1986, Paris)

Simone de Beauvoir, a French writer and feminist, was a member of the intellectual fellowship of philosopher-writers who gave literary expression to the themes of Existentialism. She is known primarily for her treatise *Le Deuxième Sexe*, 2 vol. (1949; *The Second Sex*), a scholarly and passionate plea for the abolition of what she called the myth of the "eternal feminine." This seminal work became a classic of feminist literature.

Schooled in private institutions, de Beauvoir attended the Sorbonne, where, in 1929, she passed her *agrégation* in philosophy and met Jean-Paul Sartre, beginning a lifelong association with him. She taught at a number of schools (1931–43) before turning to writing for her livelihood. In 1945 she and Sartre founded and began editing *Les Temps Modernes*, a monthly review.

Her novels expound the major Existential themes, demonstrating her conception of the writer's commitment to the times. *L'Invitée* (1943; *She Came to Stay*) describes the subtle destruction of a couple's relationship brought about by a young girl's prolonged stay in their home; it also treats the difficult problem of the relationship of a conscience to "the other," each individual conscience being fundamentally a predator to another. Of her other works of fiction, perhaps the best known is *Les Mandarins* (1954; *The Mandarins*), for which she won the Prix Goncourt. It is a chronicle of the attempts of post-World War II intellectuals to leave their "mandarin" (educated elite) status and engage in political activism. She also wrote four books of philosophy, including *Pour une Morale de l'ambiguité* (1947; *The Ethics of Ambiguity*); travel books on China (*La Longue Marche: essai sur la Chine* [1957]; *The Long March*) and the United States (*L'Amérique au jour de jour* [1948]; *America Day by Day*); and a number of essays, some of them book-length, the best known of which is *The Second Sex*.

Several volumes of her work are devoted to autobiography. These include *Mémoires d'une jeune fille rangée* (1958; *Memoirs of a Dutiful Daughter*), *La Force de l'âge* (1960; *The Prime of Life*), *La Force des choses* (1963; *Force of Circumstance*), and *Tout compte fait* (1972; *All Said and Done*). This body of work, beyond its personal interest, constitutes a clear and telling portrait of French intellectual life from the 1930s to the 1970s.

In addition to treating feminist issues, de Beauvoir was concerned with the issue of aging, which she addressed in *Une Mort très douce* (1964; *A Very Easy Death*), on her mother's death in a hospital, and in *La Vieillesse* (1970; *Old Age*), a bitter reflection on society's indifference to the elderly. In 1981 she wrote *La Cérémonie des adieux* (*Adieux: A Farewell to Sartre*), a painful account of Sartre's last years. *Simone de Beauvoir: A Biography*, by

Deirdre Bair, appeared in 1990.

Simone de Beauvoir revealed herself as a woman of formidable courage and integrity, whose life supported her thesis: the basic options of an individual must be made on the premises of an equal vocation for man and woman founded on a common structure of their being, independent of their sexuality.

WILLARD VAN ORMAN QUINE

(b. June 25, 1908, Akron, Ohio, U.S.—d. Dec. 25, 2000, Boston, Mass.)

Willard Van Orman Quine, an American philosopher and logician, is widely considered one of the dominant figures in Anglo-American (analytic) philosophy in the last half of the 20th century.

After studying mathematics and logic at Oberlin College (1926–30), Quine won a scholarship to Harvard University, where he completed his PhD in 1932. On a traveling fellowship to Europe in 1932–33, he met some of the leading philosophers and logicians of the day, including Rudolf Carnap and Alfred Tarski. After three years as a junior fellow at Harvard, Quine joined the faculty in 1936. From 1942 to 1945 he served as a naval intelligence officer in Washington, D.C. Promoted to full professor at Harvard in 1948, he remained there until 1978, when he retired.

Quine produced highly original and important work in several areas of philosophy, including logic, ontology, epistemology, and the philosophy of language. By the 1950s he had developed a comprehensive and systematic philosophical outlook that was naturalistic, empiricist, and behaviorist. Conceiving of philosophy as an extension of science, he rejected epistemological foundationalism, the attempt to ground knowledge of the external world in allegedly transcendent and self-validating mental experience. The proper task of a "naturalized epistemology," as he saw it, was simply to give a psychological account of how scientific knowledge is actually obtained.

Although much influenced by the Logical Positivism of Carnap and other members of the Vienna Circle, Quine famously rejected one of that group's cardinal doctrines, the analytic-synthetic distinction. According to this doctrine, there is a fundamental difference between statements such as "All bachelors are unmarried," which are true or false solely by virtue of the meanings of the terms they contain, and statements such as "All swans are white," which are true or false by virtue of nonlinguistic facts about the world. Quine argued that no coherent definition of analyticity had ever been proposed. One consequence of his view was that the truths of mathematics and logic, which the positivists had regarded as analytic, and the empirical truths of science differed only in "degree" and not kind. In keeping with his empiricism, Quine held that both the former and the latter were known through experience and were thus in principle revisable in the face of countervailing evidence.

In ontology, Quine recognized only those entities that it was necessary to postulate in order to assume that our best scientific theories are true—specifically, concrete physical objects and abstract sets, which were required by the mathematics used in many scientific disciplines. He rejected notions such as properties, propositions, and meanings as ill-defined or scientifically useless.

In the philosophy of language, Quine was known for

his behaviorist account of language learning and for his thesis of the "indeterminacy of translation." This is the view that there are always indefinitely many possible translations of one language into another, each of which is equally compatible with the totality of empirical evidence available to linguistic investigators. There is thus no "fact of the matter" about which translation of a language is correct. The indeterminacy of translation is an instance of a more general view, which Quine called "ontological relativity," that claims that for any given scientific theory there are always indefinitely many alternatives entailing different ontological assumptions but accounting for all available evidence equally well. Thus, it does not make sense to say that one theory rather than another gives a true description of the world.

Among Quine's many books are *Word and Object* (1960), *The Roots of Reference* (1974), and his autobiography, *The Time of My Life* (1985).

SIR A. J. AYER

(b. Oct. 29, 1910, London, Eng.—d. June 27, 1989, London)

A. J. Ayer was a British philosopher and educator and a leading representative of Logical Positivism through his widely read work *Language, Truth, and Logic* (1936).

Although Ayer was raised in London, both his father, a French Swiss businessman, and his mother, a Dutch citizen of Jewish ancestry, were born abroad, and Ayer grew up speaking French fluently. An extremely able, though sensitive, boy, he won a scholarship to Eton College (1923), where he excelled in classics but had no opportunity to study science, an omission that he would always regret. In 1929 he won a classics scholarship to the University of Oxford, where he also studied philosophy. His tutor, Gilbert Ryle (1900–76), soon described Ayer as "the best student I have yet been taught by."

Language, Truth, and Logic

Having secured a fellowship at the college of Christ Church, Ayer spent part of 1933 in Vienna, where he attended meetings of the Vienna Circle, a group of mostly German and Austrian philosophers and scientists who were just then beginning to attract the attention of philosophers in England and the United States. Although Ayer spoke poor German and was hardly able to take part in the discussions, he became convinced that the doctrine of Logical Positivism that the group was developing marked an important advance in the empiricist tradition, and he returned home an ardent convert. Within two and a half years he had written a manifesto for the movement, *Language, Truth, and Logic*.

In this work, following Wittgenstein and the members of the Vienna Circle, Ayer defended a verificationist theory of meaning (also called the verifiability principle), according to which an utterance is meaningful only if it expresses a proposition the truth or falsehood of which can be verified (at least in principle) through experience. He used this theory to argue that metaphysical talk about God, the cosmos, or "transcendent values" was not merely, as earlier empiricists had maintained, excessively conjectural but literally meaningless. Ayer's specific contribution was to develop this argument with unusual clearheadedness and rigor, showing how statements about the external world, other minds, and the past could be accorded sense through an analysis in verificationist terms. His argument that statements of moral evaluation, because they are unverifiable, are not descriptions of fact but merely "emotive" expressions of feeling aroused particular controversy.

Although Ayer claimed that *Language, Truth, and Logic* answered all major philosophical questions, the problems he had so confidently "solved" soon came back to haunt him. In a series of important papers and a book, *The Foundations of Empirical Knowledge* (1940), he wrestled with critics who doubted that all meaningful discourse could be analyzed in terms of sense experience.

In the years surrounding the publication of *Language, Truth, and Logic*, philosophy had to compete with more pressing concerns. Like many young men of the period, Ayer was critical of what he saw as the British government's do-nothing approach to the rise of unemployment at home and of fascism abroad. After briefly considering joining the British Communist Party, Ayer instead joined the Labour Party. An early and forthright critic of Neville Chamberlain's policy of appeasement, Ayer volunteered for the Welsh Guards as soon as war broke out. After completing officer training, he joined an intelligence unit, eventually becoming a specialist on France and the French Resistance and gaining the rank of major. His war assignments took him to New York, to Algeria, and, after the liberation of France, to the southern part of that country and to Paris.

The Problem of Knowledge

At the end of the war, Ayer at last secured an Oxford fellowship. One year later, in 1946, he was appointed Grote Professor of Mental Philosophy at University College,

London. Although little philosophy had been published in England during the war, Ayer found that the philosophical climate was now very different. Influenced by the ideas of the later Wittgenstein, which were only then becoming known outside Cambridge, a group of philosophers at Oxford, led by Gilbert Ryle and J.L. Austin (1911–60), were arguing persuasively that most philosophical problems were simply conceptual confusions resulting from philosophers' insufficient attention to the complex ways in which philosophically loaded terms and their cognates were used in ordinary speech. Although Ayer well understood the Oxford philosophers' weariness with metaphysical speculation and supported their commitment to careful conceptual analysis, he did not share their hostility toward philosophical theorizing.

The next decade and a half, until the early 1960s, was perhaps the most fruitful of Ayer's life. He transformed the University College philosophy department into one of the best in the country, rivaling those of Cambridge and even Oxford. He edited several series of books, presided over various discussion groups, developed a friendship with his hero Bertrand Russell, lectured around the world, and made lively contributions to literary journals and radio broadcasts. At the same time, he produced a series of influential papers and what was probably his most philosophically successful book, *The Problem of Knowledge* (1956).

In this work the great combative proclamations of *Language, Truth, and Logic* were replaced by a quieter treatment of skepticism. Whereas Ayer previously had in effect pursued a "reductionism" of all meaningful propositions to the sense-data by which they are verified, he now admitted that not everything can be translated into the language of the senses; instead, the constructions made on the basis of experience have their own inherent validity.

Later Years

Ayer was metropolitan in his tastes, enjoying the company of writers, actors, and politicians as much as that of philosophers. It was with some misgivings, then, that in 1959 Ayer returned to Oxford to become Wykeham Professor of Logic. As it was, his tenure there, until his retirement in 1978, proved extremely happy. In 1973 he published *The Central Questions of Philosophy*, in which he returned to familiar topics in the theory of knowledge and presented a commonsense conception of the world as a theory founded on the basis of sense-data.

The last decade of Ayer's life was troubled. In 1980 his first wife, Renee Lees, whom he had divorced in 1945, died, and one year later their daughter Valerie died suddenly of Hodgkin's disease. In 1982 he divorced his second wife, the writer Dee Wells. His third wife, Vanessa Lawson (formerly married to Nigel Lawson, the chancellor of the Exchequer), died in 1984, leaving him bereft. Suffering from emphysema, he collapsed in 1988 and underwent a remarkable near-death experience, in which, as he later described, he seemed to encounter the "Master of the Universe" and his ministers for space and time. (His account was misunderstood by some critics as a recantation of his atheism.)

Just before his real death in 1989, Ayer remarried Dee Wells and was united with his daughter born to the Hollywood gossip columnist Sheilah Graham. It was an end in keeping with his colorful, eventful private life.

WILFRID SELLARS

(b. May 20, 1912, Ann Arbor, Mich., U.S.—d. July 2, 1989, Pittsburgh, Pa.)

Wilfrid Sellars, an American philosopher, is best known for his critique of traditional philosophical conceptions of mind and knowledge and for his uncompromising effort to explain how human reason and thought can be reconciled with the vision of nature found in science. Although he was one of the most original and influential American philosophers of the second half of the 20th century, he remains largely unknown outside academic circles.

Sellars's father, Roy Sellars, was a distinguished Canadian philosopher. After studying at the University of Michigan and the University of Buffalo, the younger Sellars was awarded a Rhodes scholarship to the University of Oxford, where he earned bachelor's (1936) and master's (1940) degrees in philosophy, politics, and economics. He was appointed assistant professor of philosophy at the University of Iowa in 1938. After serving as an intelligence officer in the U.S. Navy (1943–46), he was appointed assistant professor of philosophy at the University of Minnesota. He was professor of philosophy at Yale University from 1959 to 1963 and University Professor of Philosophy and Research Professor of Philosophy at the University of Pittsburgh from 1963 until his death.

Sellars came to prominence in 1956 with the publication of his essay *Empiricism and the Philosophy of Mind*, a critique of a conception of mind and knowledge inherited from René Descartes (1596–1650). Sellars there attacked what he called the "myth of the given," the Cartesian idea that one can have immediate and indubitable perceptual knowledge of one's own sense experiences. Sellars's ideas anticipated and contributed to the development of theories of mind, knowledge, and science that played significant roles in later debates on these topics.

Sellars was an articulate exponent of the modernist enterprise of reconciling the comprehensive picture of reality emerging from the theoretical activities of natural science with the traditional conception of human beings as morally accountable agents and subjective centers of experience. In *Philosophy and the Scientific Image of Man* (1960), he characterized this project as bringing together into one "synoptic view" two competing images of "man-in-the-world": the "scientific" image derived from the fruits of theory construction and the "manifest" image, the "framework in terms of which man encountered himself."

Sellars subscribed to a form of philosophical naturalism according to which science is the final arbiter of what exists. Entities exist if and only if they would be invoked in a complete scientific explanation of the world. His synoptic project, however, required him to develop ways of accommodating dimensions of human experience that seem initially to resist incorporation into the "scientific image." Science describes how humans do think and act, for example, but not how they ought to think and act, and this latter element therefore requires explanation if it is to be reconciled with Sellars's naturalism. His fundamental response to these challenges was to develop a sophisticated theory of conceptual roles, concretely instantiated in human conduct and transmitted by modes of social interaction, including language. He used this theory in turn to defend a form of linguistic nominalism, the denial of the real existence of universals or irreducibly mentalistic entities as the referents or meanings of linguistic expressions. Sellars also introduced the functionalist idea of explaining semantic meaning in terms of the inferential and ultimately behavioral roles played by particular linguistic expressions, a view later known as conceptual-role semantics.

Sellars's major published works, in addition to the essays mentioned above, include *Science, Perception, and Reality* (1963), *Philosophical Perspectives* (1967), *Science and Metaphysics: Variations on Kantian Themes* (1968), *Naturalism and Ontology* (1979), and *Foundations for a Metaphysics of Pure Process* (1981).

JOHN RAWLS

(b. Feb. 21, 1921, Baltimore, Md., U.S.—d. Nov. 24, 2002, Lexington, Mass.)

John Rawls was an American political and ethical philosopher. He is widely considered the most important political philosopher of the 20th century.

Rawls was the second of five children of William Lee Rawls and Anna Abell Stump. After attending an Episcopalian preparatory school, Kent School, in Connecticut, he entered Princeton University, where he earned a bachelor's degree in 1943. He enlisted in the army later that year and served with the infantry in the South Pacific until his discharge in 1945. He returned to Princeton in 1946 and earned a PhD in moral philosophy in 1950. He taught at Princeton (1950–52), Cornell University (1953–59), the Massachusetts Institute of Technology (1960–62), and finally Harvard University, where he was appointed James Bryant Conant University Professor in 1979.

In *A Theory of Justice*, Rawls defends a conception of

"justice as fairness." He holds that an adequate account of justice cannot be derived from utilitarianism, because that doctrine is consistent with intuitively undesirable forms of government in which the greater happiness of a majority is achieved by neglecting the rights and interests of a minority. Reviving the notion of a social contract, Rawls argues that justice consists of the basic principles of government that free and rational individuals would agree to in a hypothetical situation of perfect equality. In order to ensure that the principles chosen are fair, Rawls imagines a group of individuals who have been made ignorant of the social, economic, and historical circumstances from which they come, as well as their basic values and goals, including their conception of what constitutes a "good life." Situated behind this "veil of ignorance," they could not be influenced by self-interested desires to benefit some social groups (i.e., the groups they belong to) at the expense of others. Thus they would not know any facts about their race, sex, age, religion, social or economic class, wealth, income, intelligence, abilities, talents, and so on.

In this "original position," as Rawls characterizes it, any group of individuals would be led by reason and self-interest to agree to the following principles: (1) Each person is to have an equal right to the most extensive basic liberty compatible with a similar liberty for others, and (2) Social and economic inequalities are to be arranged so that they are both (*a*) to the greatest benefit of the least advantaged and (*b*) attached to offices and positions open to all under conditions of fair equality of opportunity.

The "basic liberty" mentioned in principle 1 comprises most of the rights and liberties traditionally associated with liberalism and democracy: freedom of thought and conscience, freedom of association, the right to representative government, the right to form and join political parties, the right to personal property, and the rights and liberties necessary to secure the rule of law. Economic rights and liberties, such as freedom of contract or the right to own means of production, are not among the basic liberties as Rawls construes them. Basic liberties cannot be infringed under any circumstances, even if doing so would increase the aggregate welfare, improve economic efficiency, or augment the income of the poor.

Clause *b* of principle 2 provides that everyone has a fair and equal opportunity to compete for desirable public or private offices and positions. This entails that society must provide all citizens with the basic means necessary to participate in such competition, including appropriate education and health care. Clause *a* of principle 2 is known as the "difference principle": it requires that any unequal distribution of wealth and income be such that those who are worst off are better off than they would be under any other distribution consistent with principle 1, including an equal distribution. (Rawls holds that some inequality of wealth and income is probably necessary in order to maintain high levels of productivity.)

In Rawls's view, Soviet-style communism is unjust because it is incompatible with most basic liberties and because it does not provide everyone with a fair and equal opportunity to obtain desirable offices and positions. Pure laissez-faire capitalism is also unjust, because it tends to produce an unjust distribution of wealth and income (concentrated in the hands of a few), which in turn effectively deprives some (if not most) citizens of the basic means necessary to compete fairly for desirable offices and positions. A just society, according to Rawls, would be a "property-owning democracy" in which ownership of the means of production is widely distributed and those who are worst off are prosperous enough to be economically independent.

THOMAS S. KUHN

(b. July 18, 1922, Cincinnati, Ohio, U.S.—d. June 17, 1996, Cambridge, Mass.)

Thomas S. Kuhn was an American philosopher and historian of science who is noted for *The Structure of Scientific Revolutions* (1962), one of the most influential works of history and philosophy written in the 20th century.

Kuhn earned bachelor's (1943) and master's (1946) degrees in physics at Harvard University but obtained his PhD (1949) there in the history of science. He taught the history or philosophy of science at Harvard (1951–56), the University of California at Berkeley (1956–64), Princeton University (1964–79), and the Massachusetts Institute of Technology (1979–91).

In his first book, *The Copernican Revolution* (1957), Kuhn studied the development of the heliocentric theory of the solar system during the Renaissance. In his landmark second book, *The Structure of Scientific Revolutions*, he argued that scientific research and thought are defined by "paradigms," or conceptual world-views, that consist of formal theories, classic experiments, and trusted methods. Scientists typically accept a prevailing paradigm and try to extend its scope by refining theories, explaining puzzling data, and establishing more precise measures of standards and phenomena. Eventually, however, their efforts may generate insoluble theoretical problems or experimental anomalies that expose a paradigm's inadequacies or contradict it altogether. This accumulation of difficulties triggers a crisis that can only be resolved by an intellectual revolution that replaces an old paradigm with a new one. The overthrow of Ptolemaic cosmology by Copernican heliocentrism, and the displacement of Newtonian mechanics by quantum physics and general relativity, are both examples of major paradigm shifts.

Kuhn questioned the traditional conception of scientific progress as a gradual, cumulative acquisition of knowledge based on rationally chosen experimental frameworks. Instead, he argued that the paradigm determines the kinds of experiments scientists perform, the types of questions they ask, and the problems they consider important. A shift in the paradigm alters the fundamental concepts underlying research and inspires new standards of evidence, new research techniques, and new pathways of theory and experiment that are radically incommensurate with the old ones.

Kuhn's book revolutionized the history and philosophy of science, and his concept of paradigm shifts was extended to such disciplines as political science, economics, sociology, and even to business management. Kuhn's later works were a collection of essays, *The Essential Tension* (1977), and the technical study *Black-Body Theory and the Quantum Discontinuity* (1978).

MICHEL FOUCAULT

(b. Oct. 15, 1926, Poitiers, France—d. June 25, 1984, Paris)

Michel Foucault was a French philosopher and historian and one of the most influential and controversial scholars of the post-World War II period.

The son and grandson of a physician, Michel Foucault was born to a solidly bourgeois family. A distinguished but sometimes erratic student, Foucault gained entry at the age of 20 to the École Normale Supérieure (ENS) in Paris in 1946. After graduating in 1952, Foucault first taught at the University of Lille, then spent five years (1955–60) as a cultural attaché in Uppsala, Sweden; Warsaw, Poland; and Hamburg, West Germany (now Germany). He defended his doctoral dissertation at the ENS in 1961. Circulated under the title *Folie et déraison: histoire de la folie à l'âge classique* ("Madness and Unreason: A History of Madness in the Classical Age"), it won critical praise but a limited audience. (An abridged version was translated into English and published in 1965 as *Madness and Civilization: A History of Insanity in the Age of Reason*.)

Foucault's other early monographs, written while he taught at the University of Clermont-Ferrand in France (1960–66), had much the same fate. Not until the appearance of *Les Mots et les choses* ("Words and Things"; Eng. trans. *The Order of Things*) in 1966 did Foucault begin to attract wide notice as one of the most original and controversial thinkers of his day. He chose to watch his reputation grow from a distance—at the University of Tunis in Tunisia (1966–68). In 1969 he published *L'Archéologie du savoir* (*The Archaeology of Knowledge*). In 1970, after a brief tenure as director of the philosophy department at the University of Paris, Vincennes, he was awarded a chair in the history of systems of thought at the Collège de France, France's most prestigious post-secondary institution.

Between 1971 and 1984 Foucault wrote several works, including *Surveiller et punir: naissance de la prison* (1975; *Discipline and Punish: The Birth of the Prison*), a monograph on the emergence of the modern prison; three volumes of a history of Western sexuality; and numerous essays. Foucault was a visiting lecturer at the University of California at Berkeley for several years. He died of a septicemia typical of AIDS in 1984, the fourth volume of his history of sexuality still incomplete.

Foucault's Ideas

What types of human beings are there? What is their essence? What is the essence of human history? Of humankind? Contrary to so many of his intellectual predecessors, Foucault sought not to answer these traditional and seemingly straightforward questions but to critically examine them and the responses they had inspired. He directed his most sustained skepticism toward those responses—among them, race, the unity of reason or the psyche, progress, and liberation—that had become commonplaces in Europe and the United States in the 19th century. He argued that such commonplaces informed both Hegelian phenomenology and Marxist materialism. He argued that they also informed the evolutionary biology, physical anthropology, clinical medicine, psychology, sociology, and criminology of the same period. The latter three disciplines are part of what came to be called in French *les sciences humaines*, or "the human sciences."

Several of the philosophers of the Anglo-American positivist tradition, among them Carl Hempel, had faulted the human sciences for failing to achieve the conceptual and methodological rigor of mathematics or physics. Foucault found fault with them as well, but he decisively rejected the positivist tenet that the methods of the pure or natural sciences provided an exclusive standard for arriving at genuine or legitimate knowledge. His critique concentrated instead upon the fundamental point of reference that had grounded and guided inquiry in the human sciences: the concept of "man." The man of this inquiry was a creature purported, like many preceding conceptions, to have a constant essence—indeed, a double essence. On one hand, man was an object, like any other object in the natural world, obedient to the indiscriminate dictates of physical laws. On the other hand, man was a subject, an agent uniquely capable of comprehending and altering his worldly condition in order to become more fully, more essentially, himself. Foucault reviewed the historical record for evidence that such a creature actually had ever existed, but to no avail. Looking for objects, he found only a plurality of subjects whose features varied dramatically with shifts of place and time.

Foucault understood the very possibility of his own critique to be evidence that the concept of man was beginning to loosen its grip on Western thought. Yet a further puzzle remained: How could such an erroneous, such an impossible, figure have been so completely taken for granted for so long? Foucault's solution emphasized that in the emerging nation-states of 17th- and 18th-century Europe, "man" was a conceptual prerequisite for the creation of social institutions and practices that were then necessary to maintain an optimally productive citizenry. With the advent of "man," the notion that human character and experience were immutable gradually gave way to the notion that both body and soul could be manipulated and reformed. The latter notion lent the technologies of modern policing their enduring rationale.

Although this discipline operated on individuals, it

was paired with a current of reformism that took not individuals but various human populations as its basic object. The prevailing sensibility of its greatest champions was markedly medical. They scrutinized everything from sexual behavior to social organization for relative pathology or health. They also sought out the "deviant," but less in order to eradicate it than to keep it in acceptable check. This "biopolitics" of the reformers, according to Foucault, contained the basic principles of the modern welfare state.

For Foucault, domination was not the only outcome of these dynamics. Another was "subjectivation," the historically specific classification and shaping of individual human beings into "subjects" of various kinds—including heroic and ordinary, "normal" and "deviant." The distinction between the two came somewhat late to Foucault, but once he made and refined it he was able to clarify the status of some of his earliest observations and to identify a theme that had been present in all his writings. His understanding of subjectivation, however, changed significantly over the course of two decades, as did the methods he applied to its analysis. Intent on devising a properly specific history of subjects, he initially pressed the analogy between the corpus of statements about subjects produced and presumed true at any given historical moment and the artifacts of some archaeological site or complex. This "archaeology of knowledge" nevertheless had its shortcomings. Among other things, its consideration of both power and power-knowledge was at best partial, if not oblique.

By 1971 Foucault had already demoted "archaeology" in favor of "genealogy," a method that traced the ensemble of historical contingencies, accidents, and illicit relations that made up the ancestry of one or another currently accepted theory or concept in the human sciences. With genealogy, Foucault set out to unearth the artificiality of the dividing line between the putatively illegitimate and its putatively normal and natural opposite. *Discipline and Punish* was his genealogical exposé of the artifices of power-knowledge that had resulted in the naturalization of the "criminal character," and the first volume of *Histoire de la sexualité* (1976; *The History of Sexuality*) was his exposé of the Frankensteinian machinations that had resulted in the naturalization of the dividing line between the "homosexual" and the "heterosexual."

NOAM CHOMSKY

(b. Dec. 7, 1928, Philadelphia, Pa., U.S.)

Noam Chomsky is an American linguist and political activist whose theories of language have revolutionized the field of linguistics and exerted a profound influence on philosophy, psychology, and cognitive science.

Chomsky was introduced to linguistics by his father, a scholar of Hebrew. He studied under the linguist Zellig S. Harris at the University of Pennsylvania, where he earned bachelor's (1949) and master's (1951) degrees. Many elements of his early theories of language appear in his manuscript *Logical Structure of Linguistic Theory* (published 1975), which he wrote while a Junior Fellow at Harvard University in 1951–55. A chapter of this work, "Transformational Analysis," formed his University of Pennsylvania PhD dissertation (1955). After receiving his degree, he joined the faculty of the Massachusetts Institute of Technology (MIT), where he became a full professor in 1961. He was appointed Ferrari P. Ward

Throughout his career, Noam Chomsky has been a respected political commentator and an unflagging advocate of free speech.

Professor of Modern Languages and Linguistics in 1966 and Institute Professor in 1976.

In the 1940s and '50s the study of linguistics in the United States was dominated by the school of American structuralism. According to the structuralists, the proper object of study for linguistics is the corpus of sounds of a given language, which they call "primary linguistic data." The task of the linguist is to construct a grammar of the language by applying to the primary linguistic data a series of complex analyses that would isolate the significant units of sound in the language (phonemes) and identify their permissible combinations into words and ultimately sentences. In keeping with their strict empiricism, the structuralists argued that in order to be genuinely scientific the grammar must be mechanically extractable by these analyses from the primary linguistic data and must not include reference to unverifiable and mysterious mental entities such as "meanings." For similar reasons, structuralists proposed or were sympathetic to behaviorist accounts of language learning, in which linguistic knowledge amounts to merely a set of dispositions, or habits, acquired through conditioning and without the aid of any language-specific mental structures.

In contrast to structuralism, Chomsky's approach, as outlined in his first major publication, *Syntactic Structures* (1957), and refined considerably in several works since then, is thoroughly mentalistic, insofar as it takes the proper object of study for linguistics to be the mentally represented grammars that constitute the native speaker's knowledge of his language and the biologically innate "language faculty," or Universal Grammar, that allows the (developmentally normal) language learner as a child to construct a rich, detailed, and accurate grammar of the language to which he is exposed. Children acquire languages in relatively little time, with little or no instruction, without apparent difficulty, and on the basis of primary linguistic data that are necessarily incomplete and frequently defective. (Once they reach fluency, children routinely produce sentences they have never heard before, and many of the sentences produced by adults in their environment contain errors of various kinds, such as slurs, false starts, run-on sentences, and so on.)

These facts, according to Chomsky, demonstrate the inadequacy of behaviorist theories of language learning, which typically do not postulate mental structures beyond those representing simple induction and other "general learning strategies." Given the primary linguistic data to which speakers are exposed, it is impossible on behaviorist assumptions to construct a "descriptively adequate" grammar—i.e., a grammar that generates all and only the sentences of the language in question. The ultimate goal of linguistic science for Chomsky is to develop a theory of Universal Grammar that is "explanatorily adequate" in the sense of providing a descriptively adequate grammar for any natural language given exposure to primary linguistic data.

Chomsky's work in linguistics hastened the decline of behaviorism in psychology, prompted a revival of interest in rationalist theories of knowledge in philosophy, and spurred research into the innate rule systems that may underlie other domains of human thought and knowledge.

Chomsky is also known around the world as a political activist, though his views have received little attention in the mass media of the United States. Since the 1960s he has written numerous works and delivered countless lectures and interviews on what he considers the antidemocratic character of corporate power and its insidious effects on U.S. politics and foreign policy, the mass media, and the behavior of intellectuals.

JÜRGEN HABERMAS

(b. June 18, 1929, Düsseldorf, Ger.)

Jürgen Habermas is the most important German philosopher of the second half of the 20th century.

Habermas grew up in Gummersbach, Germany. At age 10 he joined the Hitler Youth, as did many of his contemporaries, and at age 15, during the last months of World War II, he was sent to the Western Front. After the Nazi defeat in May 1945, he completed his secondary education and attended the Universities of Bonn, Göttingen, and Zürich. At Bonn he received a PhD in philosophy in 1954 with a dissertation on Friedrich Schelling. From 1956 to 1959 he worked as Theodor Adorno's first assistant at the Institute for Social Research. Habermas left the institute in 1959 and completed his second doctorate (his habilitation thesis, which qualified him to teach at the university level) in 1961 under the political scientist Wolfgang Abendroth at the University of Marburg. His thesis was published with additions in 1962 as *Strukturwandel der Öffentlichkeit* (*The Structural Transformation of the Public Sphere*).

In 1961 Habermas became a *privatdozent* (unsalaried professor and lecturer) in Marburg, and in 1962 he was named extraordinary professor (professor without chair) at the University of Heidelberg. He succeeded Max Horkheimer as professor of philosophy and sociology at the Johann Wolfgang Goethe University of Frankfurt

Jürgen Habermas is a renowned German intellectual who has had a worldwide impact on philosophy and the social sciences.

am Main (Frankfurt University) in 1964. After 10 years as director of the Max Planck Institute in Starnberg (1971–81), he returned to Frankfurt, where he retired in 1994. Thereafter he taught in the United States at Northwestern University (Evanston, Illinois) and New York University and lectured worldwide.

Philosophy and Social Theory

In his 1965 inaugural lecture at Frankfurt University, *Erkenntnis und Interesse* (1965; *Knowledge and Human Interests*), and in the book of the same title published three years later, Habermas set forth the foundations of a normative version of critical social theory, the Marxist social theory developed by Horkheimer, Adorno, and other members of the Frankfurt Institute from the 1920s onward. He did this on the basis of a general theory of human interests, according to which different areas of human knowledge and inquiry—e.g., the physical, biological, and social sciences—are expressions of distinct, but equally basic, human interests. These basic interests are in turn unified by reason's overarching pursuit of its own freedom, which is expressed in scholarly disciplines that are critical of unfree modes of social life. In his rethinking of the foundations of early critical social theory, Habermas sought to unite the philosophical traditions of Karl Marx and German idealism with the psychoanalysis of Sigmund Freud and the pragmatism of the American logician and philosopher Charles Sanders Peirce.

Habermas took a linguistic-communicative turn in *Theorie des kommunikativen Handelns* (1981; *The Theory of Communicative Action*). He argued that human interaction in one of its fundamental forms is "communicative" rather than "strategic" in nature, insofar as it is aimed at mutual understanding and agreement rather than at the achievement of the self-interested goals of individuals. Such understanding and agreement, however, are possible only to the extent that the communicative interaction in which individuals take part resists all forms of nonrational coercion. The notion of an "ideal communication community" functions as a guide that can be formally applied both to regulate and to critique concrete speech situations. Using this regulative and critical ideal, individuals would be able to raise, accept, or reject each other's claims to truth, rightness, and sincerity solely on the basis of the "unforced force" of the better argument—i.e., on the basis of reason and evidence—and all participants would be motivated solely by the desire to obtain mutual understanding. Although the ideal communication community is never perfectly realized (which is why Habermas appeals to it as a regulative or critical ideal rather than as a concrete historical community), the projected horizon of unconstrained communicative action within it can serve as a model of free and open public discussion within liberal-democratic societies. Likewise, this type of regulative and critical ideal can serve as a justification of deliberative liberal-democratic political institutions, because it is only within such institutions that unconstrained communicative action is possible.

Liberal democracy is not a guarantee that communicative rationality will flourish, however. Indeed, in modern capitalist societies, social institutions that ideally should be communicative in character—e.g., family, politics, and education—have come to embody a merely "strategic" rationality, according to Habermas. Such institutions are increasingly overrun by economic and bureaucratic forces that are guided not by an ideal of mutual understanding but rather by principles of administrative power and economic efficiency.

Habermas's findings carried wide-ranging normative implications. In *Moralbewusstsein und kommunikatives Handeln* (1983; *Moral Consciousness and Communicative Action*), he elaborated a general theory of "discourse ethics," or "communicative ethics," which concerns the ethical presuppositions of ideal communication that would have to be invoked in an ideal communication community.

Habermas was criticized by both the postmodern left and the neoconservative right for his trust in the power of rational discussion to resolve major domestic and international conflicts. Habermas responded to critics at both ends of the political spectrum by developing a more robust communicative theory of democracy, law, and constitutions in *Faktizität und Geltung* (1992; *Between Facts and Norms*) and other works. In *Zeit der Ubergänge* (2001; *Time of Transitions*), he offered global democratic alternatives to wars that employ terrorism as well as to the "war on terrorism."

SIR BERNARD WILLIAMS

(b. Sept. 21, 1929, Westcliff, Essex, Eng.—d. June 10, 2003, Rome, Italy)

Bernard Williams was an English philosopher who is noted especially for his writings on ethics and the history of Western philosophy, both ancient and modern.

Williams was educated at Chigwell School, Essex, and Balliol College, Oxford. During the 1950s he served in the Royal Air Force (1951–53) and was a fellow of All

Souls College and New College, Oxford. He was appointed Knightbridge Professor of Philosophy at the University of Cambridge in 1967 and Provost of King's College, Cambridge, in 1979. He was Monroe Deutsch Professor of Philosophy at the University of California, Berkeley, from 1988 to 2003 and White's Professor of Moral Philosophy at Oxford from 1990 to 1996.

In 1955 Williams married Shirley Catlin, who, as Shirley Williams, became a prominent political figure in Britain; in 1993 she was created Baroness Williams of Crosby. In 1974 the marriage was dissolved, and Williams married Patricia Skinner. Williams headed or served on a number of public commissions, notably the Committee on Obscenity and Film Censorship (1977–79), and was a director of the English National Opera. He was knighted in 1999.

Philosophy as a Humanistic Discipline

Williams was trained in classics and wrote memorably about Plato, Aristotle, and Greek moral consciousness, but he was also one of the most prolific and versatile philosophers of his time. His published works include writings on René Descartes (1596–1650), Friedrich Nietzsche (1844–1900), and Ludwig Wittgenstein (1889–1951) and important papers and books on personal identity, the relation of morality to human motivation, the idea of social and political equality, the nature and value of truth, the significance of death, and the role and limits of objectivity in science, morality, and human life. He did not put forward a systematic philosophical theory; indeed, he was suspicious of systematic theories, particularly in ethics, because, in his view, they failed to be true to the contingency, complexity, and individuality of human life.

Williams was recognized for his brilliance even as an undergraduate. He was trained in philosophy when Oxford was home to the new movement of linguistic analysis, or ordinary language philosophy, led by J. L. Austin, but the breadth of his cultural, historical, and political interests kept him from becoming an adherent of that school. He met its standards of clarity of expression and rigor in argument, but his aims in philosophy went far beyond conceptual analysis. He regarded philosophy as an effort to achieve a deeper understanding of human life and the human point of view in its multiple dimensions. For the same reasons, he also resisted the tendency to regard scientific knowledge as the model of understanding to which philosophy should aspire at a more abstract level—a tendency that was strengthened during his lifetime by the growing influence of the American philosopher W.V.O. Quine and by a shift in the center of gravity of English-language philosophy from Britain to the United States. Williams held that physical science could aspire to an objectivity and universality that did not make sense for humanistic subjects, and his greatest influence came from his challenge to the ambition of universality and objectivity in ethics, especially as expressed in utilitarianism but also in the tradition established by Immanuel Kant.

The Absolute Conception of Reality

In his book *Descartes: The Project of Pure Inquiry* (1978), Williams gave a compelling description of the ideal of objectivity in science, which he called the "absolute conception" of reality. According to this conception, different human perspectives on and representations of the world are the product of interaction between human beings, as constituents of the world, and the world itself as an independently existing reality. Humans cannot apprehend the world except by some form of perception or representation; yet they can recognize, and to some extent identify and try to compensate for, the distortions or limitations that their own point of view and their relation to the rest of reality introduce. The aim of objectivity in science is by this method to approach as closely as possible to the absolute conception—a conception of what is there "anyway," independent of the human point of view. Historical self-consciousness about the contingent elements in this process is compatible with the idea of a single truth toward which humans are trying to make progress.

Williams was cognizant of the doubts that exist regarding whether this ideal is intelligible, let alone attainable, in light of the fact that human thinking must start from some particular historical moment and must use the contingent biological faculties and cultural tools that happen to be at hand. But whatever may be the difficulties in pursuing this ideal, he believed that it makes sense as an ambition. If there is a way things are anyway, then it makes sense to want to know what that way is and to explain the nature of human perceptions in terms of it.

Morality and the Limits of Objectivity

Some philosophers, in the tradition of David Hume (1711–76), have denied that there can be objective truth in ethics on the ground that this would have to mean, very implausibly, that moral propositions are true because they represent moral entities or structures that are part of the furniture of the world—moral realities with which humans have some kind of causal interaction, as they do with the physical objects of scientific knowledge. Williams was also doubtful about objectivity in ethics, but his criticism does not depend on this false analogy with science and is more interesting.

Moral judgments, according to Williams, are about what people should do and how they should live; they do not at all purport to represent how things are in the outside world. So, if there is any objectivity in moral judgments, it would have to be sought in a different analogy with scientific objectivity. Objective truth in ethics would have to consist not in ethical entities or properties added to the absolute conception of the external world but in the objective validity of the reasoning that supports certain practical, rather than descriptive, judgments about what people should do and how they should live. The analogy with scientific objectivity would reside in the fact that the way to arrive at such objective and universally valid truth would be to detect and correct for the biases and distortions introduced into one's practical judgment by contingencies of one's personal or parochial perspective. The more distortions one could correct, the closer one would get to the truth.

But it is just this aim, central to the idea of moral objectivity, that Williams thinks is fundamentally misguided. Williams finds something bizarre about the theoretical ambition of discovering a standard for practical judgment that escapes the perspectival peculiarities of the individual point of view. This applies to any ethical theory with a strong basis in impartiality or with a claim to universal validity. Williams's basic point is that, in the practical domain, the ambition of transcending one's own point of view is absurd. If taken seriously, it is likely to be profoundly self-deceived in its application. To Williams, the ambition is akin to that of the person who tries to eliminate from his life all traces of the fact that it is his.

Williams developed this objection through his general view that practical reasons must be "internal" rather than "external": that is, reasons for action must derive from motives that a person already has; they cannot create new motives by themselves, through the force of reason alone. He also defended a limited form of ethical relativism. He believed that, while there can be ethical truth, it is local and historically contingent and based on reasons deriving from people's actual motives and practices, which are not timeless or universal. Consequently, moral judgments cannot be applied to cultures too far removed in time and character from the culture in which they originate.

These arguments appear in *Ethics and the Limits of Philosophy* (1985), *A Critique of Utilitarianism* (1973; in *Utilitarianism: For and Against*), and some of the essays reprinted in *Moral Luck* (1981) and *Making Sense of Humanity* (1995). The debate provoked by Williams's claim that impersonal moral standards undermine the integrity of personal projects and personal relations, which give life its very meaning, was an important part of the moral and political philosophy of the later 20th century. Even philosophers who did not accept Williams's conclusions were in most cases led to recognize the importance of accommodating the personal point of view as a factor in moral theory.

Williams also raised and explored the deep question of whether a person's moral status is immune to "luck," or purely contingent circumstances, as Kant had argued (for Kant, the moral status of an individual depends only on the quality of his will). Williams invented the concept of "moral luck" and offered strong reasons to think that people are morally vulnerable to contingencies beyond their control, a conception he found exemplified in Greek tragedy. Oedipus, for example, is not relieved of guilt for killing his father and marrying his mother by the fact that he did not know at the time that that was what he was doing. Williams's remarkable philosophical-literary-historical work, *Shame and Necessity* (1993), presented these ideas in a rich study of Greek ethical thought.

Williams came to the conclusion that, instead of following the model of natural science, the project of understanding human nature should rely on history, which provides some distance from the perspective of the present without leaving the fullness of the human perspective behind. During the later part of his career, this viewpoint coincided with his admiration for Nietzsche, whose genealogical method was an example of historical self-exploration. In Williams's last book, *Truth and Truthfulness* (2002), he applied these ideas to the importance of truth in the theoretical and practical spheres as well as in political and personal relations.

Williams's major published works, in addition to those mentioned above, include *Morality: An Introduction to Ethics* (1972); *Problems of the Self: Philosophical Papers* (1973); *In the Beginning Was the Deed: Realism and Moralism in Political Argument* (2005); *The Sense of the Past: Essays in the History of Philosophy* (2005); *Philosophy as a Humanistic Discipline* (2005); and *On Opera* (2006).

JACQUES DERRIDA

(b. July 15, 1930, El Biar, Alg.—d. Oct. 8, 2004, Paris, France)

Jacques Derrida was a French philosopher who developed a technique of philosophical and literary analysis known as deconstruction. His critique of Western philosophy and analyses of the nature of language, writing, and meaning were highly controversial yet immensely influential in much of the intellectual world in the late 20th century.

Derrida was born to Sephardic Jewish parents in French-governed Algeria. Educated in the French tradition, he went to France in 1949, studied at the elite École Normale Supérieure (ENS), and taught philosophy at the Sorbonne (1960–64), the ENS (1964–84), and the École des Hautes Études en Sciences Sociales (1984–99), all in Paris. From the 1960s he published numerous books and essays on an immense range of topics and taught and lectured throughout the world, including at Yale University and the University of California, Irvine, attaining an international celebrity comparable only to that of Jean-Paul Sartre a generation earlier.

Derrida is most celebrated as the principal exponent of deconstruction, a term he coined for the critical examination of the fundamental conceptual distinctions, or "oppositions," inherent in Western philosophy since the time of the ancient Greeks. These oppositions are characteristically "binary" and "hierarchical," involving a pair of terms in which one member of the pair is assumed to be primary or fundamental, the other secondary or derivative. Examples include nature and culture, speech and writing, mind and body, presence and absence, inside and outside, literal and metaphorical, intelligible and sensible, and form and meaning, among many others. To "deconstruct" an opposition is to explore the tensions and contradictions between the hierarchical ordering assumed or asserted in the text and other aspects of the text's meaning, especially those that are indirect or implicit. Such an analysis shows that the opposition is not natural or necessary but a product, or "construction," of the text itself.

The speech/writing opposition, for example, is manifested in texts that treat speech as a more authentic form of language than writing. These texts assume that the speaker's ideas and intentions are directly expressed and immediately "present" in speech, whereas in writing they are comparatively remote or "absent" and thus more easily misunderstood. As Derrida points out, however, speech functions as language only to the extent that it shares characteristics traditionally assigned to writing, such as absence, "difference," and the possibility of misunderstanding. This fact is indicated by philosophical texts themselves, which invariably describe speech in terms of examples and metaphors drawn from writing, even in cases where writing is explicitly claimed to be secondary to speech. Significantly, Derrida does not wish simply to invert the speech/writing opposition—i.e., to show that writing is really prior to speech. As with any deconstructive analysis, the point is to restructure, or "displace," the opposition so as to show that neither term is primary.

The speech/writing opposition derives from a pervasive picture of meaning that equates linguistic meaning with the ideas and intentions in the mind of the speaker or author. Building on theories of the Swiss linguist Ferdinand de Saussure, Derrida coined the term *différance*, meaning both a difference and an act of deferring, to characterize the way in which linguistic meaning is created rather than given. For Derrida as for Saussure, the meaning of a word is a function of the distinctive contrasts it displays with other, related meanings. Because each word depends for its meaning on the meanings of other words, it follows that the meaning of a word is never fully "present" to us, as it would be if meanings were the same as ideas or intentions; instead it is endlessly "deferred" in an infinitely long chain of meanings. Derrida expresses this idea by saying that meaning is created by the "play" of differences between words—a play that is "limitless," "infinite," and "indefinite."

In the 1960s Derrida's work was welcomed in France and elsewhere by thinkers interested in the broad interdisciplinary movement known as structuralism. The structuralists analyzed various cultural phenomena—such as myths, religious rituals, literary narratives, and fashions in dress and adornment—as general systems of signs analogous to natural languages, with their own vocabularies and their own underlying rules and structures, and attempted to develop a metalanguage of terms and concepts in which the various sign systems could be described. Some of Derrida's early work was a critique of major structuralist thinkers such as Saussure, the anthropologist Claude Lévi-Strauss, and the intellectual historian and philosopher Michel Foucault. Derrida was thus seen, especially in the United States, as leading a movement beyond structuralism to "poststructuralism," which was skeptical about the possibility of a general science of meaning.

RICHARD RORTY

(b. Oct. 4, 1931, New York, N.Y., U.S.—d. June 8, 2007, Palo Alto, Calif.)

Richard Rorty was an American pragmatist philosopher and public intellectual. He is remembered for his wide-ranging critique of the modern conception of philosophy as a quasi-scientific enterprise aimed at reaching certainty and objective truth. In politics he argued against programs of both the left and the right in favor of what he described as a meliorative and reformist "bourgeois liberalism."

The son of nonacademic leftist intellectuals who broke with the American Communist Party in the early 1930s, Rorty attended the University of Chicago and Yale University, where he obtained a PhD in 1956. Following two years in the army, he taught philosophy at Wellesley College (1958–61) and Princeton University (1961–82) before accepting a position in the department of humanities at the University of Virginia. From 1998 until his retirement in 2005, Rorty taught comparative literature at Stanford University.

Rorty's views are somewhat easier to characterize in negative than in positive terms. In epistemology he opposed foundationalism, the view that all knowledge can be grounded, or justified, in a set of basic statements that do not themselves require justification. According to his "epistemological behaviorism," Rorty held that no statement is epistemologically more basic than any other, and no statement is ever justified "finally" but only relative to some circumscribed and contextually determined set of additional statements. In the philosophy of language, Rorty rejected the idea that sentences or beliefs are "true" or "false" in any interesting sense other than being useful or successful within a broad social practice. He also opposed representationism, the view that the main function of language is to represent or picture pieces of an objectively existing reality. Finally, in metaphysics he rejected both realism and antirealism, or idealism, as products of mistaken representationalist assumptions about language.

Because Rorty did not believe in certainty or absolute truth, he did not advocate the philosophical pursuit of such things. Instead, he believed that the role of philosophy is to conduct an intellectual "conversation" between contrasting but equally valid forms of intellectual inquiry—including science, literature, politics, religion, and many others—with the aim of achieving mutual understanding and resolving conflicts. This general view is reflected in Rorty's political works, which consistently defend traditional left-liberalism and criticize newer forms of "cultural leftism" as well as more conservative positions.

Rorty defended himself against charges of relativism and subjectivism by claiming that he rejected the crucial distinctions these doctrines presuppose. His publications include *Philosophy and the Mirror of Nature* (1979), *Consequences of Pragmatism* (1982), and *Contingency, Irony, and Solidarity* (1989).

RICHARD NOZICK

(b. Nov. 16, 1938, Brooklyn, N.Y., U.S.—d. Jan. 23, 2002, Cambridge, Mass.)

The American philosopher Richard Nozick is best known for his rigorous defense of libertarianism in his first major work, *Anarchy, State, and Utopia* (1974). A wide-ranging thinker, Nozick also made important contributions to epistemology, the problem of personal identity, and decision theory.

Nozick was the only child of Max Nozick, a Russian immigrant and businessman, and Sophie Cohen Nozick. After attending public school in Brooklyn, Nozick enrolled at Columbia College, where he earned a bachelor's degree in philosophy in 1959. He received a PhD in philosophy at Princeton University in 1963, having written a dissertation on decision theory under Carl Hempel. He taught at Princeton (1962–65), Harvard University (1965–67), and Rockefeller University (1967–69). In 1969, when he was 30 years old, he returned to Harvard as one of the youngest full professors in the university's history. He remained at Harvard for the remainder of his teaching career.

Conversion to Libertarianism

During his high school and college years, Nozick was a member of the student New Left and an enthusiastic socialist. At Columbia he helped to found a campus branch of the League for Industrial Democracy, a precursor of the Students for a Democratic Society. While in graduate school he read works by libertarian thinkers such as F.A. Hayek and Ludwig von Mises, and his political views began to change.

His conversion to libertarianism culminated in 1974 with the publication of *Anarchy, State, and Utopia*, a closely argued and highly original defense of the libertarian "minimal state" and a critique of the social-democratic liberalism of his Harvard colleague John Rawls. Immediately hailed by conservative intellectuals, the work became a kind of philosophical manifesto of the New Right, though Nozick himself was not entirely comfortable with this association.

The Minimal State

The main purpose of *Anarchy, State, and Utopia* is to show that the minimal state, and only the minimal state, is morally justified. By a minimal state Nozick means a state that functions essentially as a "night watchman," with powers limited to those necessary to protect citizens against violence, theft, and fraud. By arguing that the minimal state is justified, Nozick seeks to refute anarchism, which opposes any state whatsoever. By arguing that no more than the minimal state is justified, Nozick seeks to refute modern forms of liberalism, as well as socialism and other leftist ideologies.

Against anarchism, Nozick claims that a minimal state is justified because it (or something very much like it) would arise spontaneously among people living in a hypothetical "state of nature" through transactions that would not involve the violation of anyone's natural rights. Following the 17th-century English philosopher John Locke, Nozick assumes that everyone possesses the natural rights to life, liberty, and property, including the right to claim as property the fruits or products of one's labor and the right to dispose of one's property as one sees fit (provided that in doing so one does not violate the rights of anyone else). Everyone also has the natural right to punish those who violate or attempt to violate one's own natural rights. Because defending one's natural rights in a state of nature would be difficult for anyone to do on his own, individuals would band together to form "protection associations," in which members would work together to defend each other's rights and to punish rights violators. Eventually, some of these associations would develop into private businesses offering protection and punishment services for a fee.

The great importance that individuals would attach to such services would give the largest protection firms a natural competitive advantage, and eventually only one firm, or a confederation of firms, would control all the protection and punishment business in the community. Because this firm (or confederation of firms) would have a monopoly of force in the territory of the community and because it would protect the rights of everyone living there, it would constitute a minimal state in the libertarian sense. And because the minimal state would come about without violating anyone's natural rights, a state with at least its powers is justified.

Against liberalism and ideologies farther left, Nozick claims that no more than the minimal state is justified, because any state with more extensive powers would violate the natural rights of its citizens. Thus the state should not have the power to control prices or to set a minimum wage, because doing so would violate the natural right of citizens to dispose of their property, including their labor, as they see fit. For similar reasons, the state should not have the power to establish public education or health care through taxes imposed on citizens who may wish to spend their money on private services instead. Indeed, according to Nozick, any mandatory taxation used to fund services or benefits other than those constitutive of the minimal state is unjust, because such taxation amounts to a kind of "forced labor" for the state by those who must pay the tax.

Nozick's vision of legitimate state power thus contrasts markedly with that of Rawls and his followers. Rawls argues that the state should have whatever powers are necessary to ensure that those citizens who are least well-off are as well-off as they can be (though these powers must be consistent with a variety of basic rights and freedoms). This viewpoint is derived from Rawls's theory of justice, one principle of which is that an unequal distribution of wealth and income is acceptable only if those at the bottom are better off than they would be under any other distribution.

Nozick's response to such arguments is to claim that they rest on a false conception of distributive justice. They wrongly define a just distribution in terms of the pattern it exhibits at a given time (e.g., an equal distribution or a distribution that is unequal to a certain extent) or in terms of the historical circumstances surrounding its development (e.g., those who worked the hardest have more) rather than in terms of the nature of the transactions through which the distribution came about. For Nozick, any distribution of "holdings," as he calls them, no matter how unequal, is just if (and only if) it arises from a just distribution through legitimate means. One legitimate means is the appropriation of something that is unowned in circumstances where the acquisition would not disadvantage others. A second means is the voluntary transfer of ownership of holdings to someone else. A third means is the rectification of past injustices in the acquisition or transfer of holdings. According to Nozick, anyone who acquired what he has through these means is morally entitled to it. Thus the "entitlement" theory of justice states that the distribution of holdings in a society is just if (and only if) everyone in that society is entitled to what he has.

Nozick emphasizes that his vision of the minimal state is inclusive and compatible with the existence of smaller communities based on varying theories of justice. A group that wished to form a socialist community governed by an egalitarian theory would be free to do so, as long as it did not force others to join the community against their will. Indeed, every group would enjoy the same freedom to realize its own idea of a good society. In this way, according to Nozick, the minimal state constitutes a "framework for utopia."

Anarchy, State, and Utopia has generated an enormous

secondary literature, much of it critical. Unlike Rawls, however, Nozick did not attempt to defend or revise his political views in published work. Nozick's other books include *Philosophical Explanations* (1981), *The Nature of Rationality* (1993), and *Invariances: The Structure of the Objective World* (2001).

SAUL KRIPKE

(b. Nov. 13, 1940, Bay Shore, Long Island, N.Y., U.S.—d. Sept. 15, 2020, Plainsboro, N.J.)

Saul Kripke is an American philosopher and logician. From the 1960s he was one of the most powerful thinkers in Anglo-American (analytic) philosophy.

Kripke began his important work on the semantics of modal logic (the logic of modal notions such as necessity and possibility) while he was still a high-school student in Omaha, Nebraska. In 1962 he graduated from Harvard with the only nonhonorary degree he ever received, a BS in mathematics. He remained at Harvard until 1968, first as a member of the Harvard Society of Fellows and then as a lecturer. During these years he continued a series of publications extending his original results in modal logic; he also published important papers in intuitionistic logic (the logic underlying the mathematical intuitionism of L. E. J. Brouwer), set theory, and the theory of transfinite recursion. Kripke taught logic and philosophy at Rockefeller University from 1968 to 1976 and at Princeton University, as McCosh Professor of Philosophy, from 1976 until his retirement in 1998. He delivered the prestigious John Locke Lectures at the University of Oxford in 1973 and received the Rolf Schock Prize in logic and philosophy, awarded by the Royal Swedish Academy of Sciences, in

2001. In 2003 he was appointed distinguished professor at the City University of New York (CUNY).

Naming and Necessity

Kripke's most important philosophical publication, *Naming and Necessity* (1980), based on transcripts of three lectures he delivered at Princeton in 1970, changed the course of analytic philosophy. It provided the first cogent account of necessity and possibility as metaphysical concepts, and it distinguished both concepts from the epistemological notions of a posteriori knowledge and a priori knowledge (knowledge acquired through experience and knowledge independent of experience, respectively) and from the linguistic notions of analytic truth and synthetic truth, or truth by virtue of meaning and truth by virtue of fact. In the course of making these distinctions, Kripke revived the ancient doctrine of essentialism, according to which objects possess certain properties necessarily—without them the objects would not exist at all. On the basis of this doctrine and revolutionary new ideas about the meaning and reference of proper names and of common nouns denoting "natural kinds" (such as *heat*, *water*, and *tiger*), he argued forcefully that some propositions are necessarily true but knowable only a posteriori—e.g., "Water is H_2O" and "Heat is mean molecular kinetic energy"—and that some propositions are contingently true (true in some circumstances but not others) but knowable a priori. These arguments overturned the conventional view, inherited from Immanuel Kant (1720–1804), which identified all a priori propositions as necessary and all a posteriori propositions as contingent.

Naming and Necessity also had far-reaching

implications regarding the question of whether linguistic meaning and the contents of beliefs and other mental states are partly constituted by social and environmental facts external to the individual. According to Kripke's causal theory of reference, for example, the referent of a given use of a proper name, such as *Aristotle*, is transmitted through an indefinitely long series of earlier uses; this series constitutes a causal-historical chain that is traceable, in principle, to an original, or "baptismal," application. Kripke's view posed a serious challenge to the prevailing "description" theory, which held that the referent of a name is the individual who is picked out by an associated definite description, such as (in the case of Aristotle) *the teacher of Alexander the Great*. Finally, Kripke's work contributed greatly to the decline of ordinary language philosophy and related schools, which held that philosophy is nothing more than the logical analysis of language.

DAVID KELLOGG LEWIS

(b. Sept. 28, 1941, Oberlin, Ohio, U.S.—d. Oct. 14, 2001, Princeton, N.J.)

David Kellogg Lewis was an American philosopher who, at the time of his death, was considered by many to be the leading figure in Anglo-American (analytic) philosophy.

Both Lewis's father and his mother taught government at Oberlin College. Lewis studied philosophy at Swarthmore College (BA, 1962) and Harvard University, where he received an MA in 1964 and a PhD in 1967. His dissertation on linguistic convention, written under the supervision of Willard Van Orman Quine (1908–2000), was published as *Convention: A Philosophical Study* in 1969. Lewis taught at the University of California, Los Angeles, from 1966 to 1970 and thereafter at Princeton University. He died suddenly and unexpectedly at age 60, at the height of his intellectual powers.

In introductory essays written for two collections of his papers, Lewis identified several "recurring themes" that unify his work. Four of these themes are particularly important:

1. There are possible but nonactual things. Nonactual things do not differ from actual things in any fundamentally important way; nonactual human beings, for example, are very much like actual human beings. The largest and most inclusive nonactual things, which are not parts of any larger nonactual things, are nonactual worlds. The actual world, the object that is normally called the cosmos or the universe, and the many nonactual worlds constitute the realm of "possible worlds."

2. Temporal relations are strongly analogous to spatial relations. Just as the far side of the moon is elsewhere in space (relative to an observer on Earth), so things in the past or the future are "elsewhere in time" but are no less real for being so. Moreover, relations between actual and nonactual things are strongly analogous to temporal relations and therefore to spatial relations. All things, actual and nonactual, inhabit "logical space," and nonactual things are "elsewhere" in this space but are no less real for being so. Actual human beings correctly call the world they inhabit "actual" because it is the world they inhabit. Nonactual human beings likewise correctly call the worlds they inhabit "actual" for the same reason. The term *actual*, therefore, is strongly analogous to terms like *here* and *now*: in each case the referent of the term varies depending on the context (place, time, or

world) in which it is uttered.

3. Physical science, if successful, will provide a complete description of the actual world.

4. Given any possible world in which every inhabitant of that world is in space and time (as is the case in the actual world), everything true about that world and its inhabitants supervenes on—is determined or settled by—the distribution of "local qualities" in space and time in that world. (A local quality is a property or characteristic that can be instantiated at a specific point in space and time. Although it is ultimately up to physics to determine what local qualities there are, two likely candidates are electric charge and temperature.) Theme 3 implies that all local qualities in the actual world are physical qualities. Lewis considered it an open question whether there are nonphysical local qualities in other possible worlds.

Lewis regarded his doctrine of nonactual things and worlds as a "philosopher's paradise," and much of his work on particular philosophical problems (in metaphysics, the philosophy of language, the philosophy of mind, and epistemology) presupposed the reality of nonactual things. Few philosophers have accepted this presupposition, however; most have regarded it as simply unbelievable. Nevertheless, almost all philosophers who have studied Lewis's work have concluded that there is very little of it that cannot be detached from his doctrine of the nonactual and restated in terms of what they would consider a more plausible theory. (Lewis, it should be noted, devoted considerable effort to the attempt to show that all theories of the nonactual other than his own are unworkable.) Once so detached, they agree, Lewis's work is uniformly of great value.

PETER (ALBERT DAVID) SINGER

(b. July 6, 1946, Melbourne, Australia)

Peter Singer, an Australian ethical and political philosopher, is best known for his work in bioethics and his role as one of the intellectual founders of the modern animal rights movement.

Singer's Jewish parents emigrated to Australia from Vienna in 1938 to escape Nazi persecution following the Anschluss. Three of Singer's grandparents were subsequently killed in the Holocaust. Growing up in Melbourne, Singer attended Scotch College and the University of Melbourne, where he earned a BA in philosophy and history (1967) and an MA in philosophy (1969). In 1969 he entered the University of Oxford, receiving a B.Phil. degree in 1971 and serving as Radcliffe Lecturer in Philosophy at University College from 1971 to 1973. At Oxford his association with a vegetarian student group and his reflection on the morality of his own meat eating led him to adopt vegetarianism. While at Oxford and during a visiting professorship at New York University in 1973–74, he wrote what would become his best-known and most influential work, *Animal Liberation: A New Ethics for Our Treatment of Animals* (1975).

Returning to Australia, he lectured at La Trobe University (1975–76) and was appointed professor of philosophy at Monash University (1977). He also became director of Monash's Centre for Human Bioethics in 1983 and codirector of its Institute for Ethics and Public Policy in 1992. In 1999 he was appointed Ira W. DeCamp Professor of Bioethics in the University Center for Human Values at Princeton University. He became Laureate Professor at the Centre for Applied Philosophy and Public Ethics at the University of Melbourne in 2005.

In keeping with ethical principles that guided his thinking and writing from the 1970s, Singer devoted much of his time and effort (and a considerable portion of his income) to social and political causes, most notably animal rights but also famine and poverty relief, environmentalism, and abortion rights. By the 1990s his intellectual leadership of the increasingly successful animal rights movement and his controversial stands on some bioethical issues had made him one of the world's most widely recognized public intellectuals.

Singer's work in applied ethics and his activism in politics were informed by his utilitarianism, the tradition in ethical philosophy that holds that actions are right or wrong depending on the extent to which they promote happiness or prevent pain. In an influential early article, "Famine, Affluence, and Morality" (1972), occasioned by the catastrophic cyclone in Bangladesh in 1971, he rejected the common prephilosophical assumption that physical proximity is a relevant factor in determining one's moral obligations to others. Regarding the question of whether people in affluent countries have a greater obligation to help those near them than to contribute to famine relief in Bangladesh, he wrote: "It makes no moral difference whether the person I can help is a neighbor's child ten yards from me or a Bengali whose name I shall never know, ten thousand miles away." The only important question, according to Singer, is whether the evil that may be prevented by one's contribution outweighs whatever inconvenience or hardship may be involved in contributing—and for the large majority of people in affluent societies, the answer is clearly yes.

An interesting philosophical implication of Singer's larger argument was that the traditional distinction between duty and charity—between actions that one is obliged to do and actions that it would be good to do even though one is not obliged to do them—was seriously weakened, if not completely undermined. On the utilitarian principles Singer plausibly applied to this case, any action becomes a duty if it will prevent more pain than it causes or cause more happiness than it prevents.

The publication of *Animal Liberation* in 1975 greatly contributed to the growth of the animal rights movement by calling attention to the routine torture and abuse of countless animals in factory farms and in scientific research; at the same time, it generated significant new interest among ethical philosophers in the moral status of nonhuman animals. The most-important philosophical contribution of the book was Singer's penetrating examination of the concept of "speciesism" (which he did not invent): the idea that the species of a being should be relevant to its moral status. Speciesism is rationally unjustified, according to Singer, just as is the comparable notion that race or sex should be relevant to the moral status of a human being. Singer argues that all beings with interests (all beings who are capable of enjoyment or suffering, broadly construed) deserve to have those interests taken into account in one's moral decision making. Furthermore, the kind of consideration a being deserves should depend on the nature of the interests it has (what kinds of enjoyment or suffering it is capable of), not on the species it happens to belong to. To think otherwise is to endorse a prejudice exactly analogous to racism or sexism. Speciesism was extensively explored by ethical philosophers and eventually became a familiar theme in popular discussions of animal rights in a variety of forums.

In numerous books and articles published in the 1980s and after, Singer continued to develop his positions on animal rights and other topics in applied ethical and political philosophy—including stem cell research, infanticide, euthanasia, global environmental concerns, and the political implications of Darwinism—placing them within the context of theoretical developments in utilitarianism.

Glossary

anti-Semitism: Hatred of Jewish people.

cognizant: Aware of something.

deconstruction: The critical examination of the fundamental conceptual distinctions, or "oppositions," inherent in Western philosophy.

empiricism: The theory that experience is not only the best teacher, but the only true source of knowledge.

existentialism: A philosophy that stresses freedom of choice and responsibility for the consequences of one's actions.

fascism: A political system headed by a dictator in which opposition is not permitted.

hierarchical: Belonging to a system by which people or things are ordered by status or importance.

insoluble: Difficult to solve or explain.

linguistics: The study of language.

machination: The scheming or artful actions that are used to achieve or obtain something.

nominalism: The school of thought that denies universal concepts have any reality apart from the individual things signified by the universal or general term.

phenomenology: The quest for the essences of things.

semantic: Of or relating to the meanings of words and phrases.

utilitarianism: The belief that something's worth can be determined by how useful it is.

totalitarianism: The concept that a citizen should be controlled by the complete power of a state.

For More Information

BOOKS

Board, Tempra. *Who Are Libertarians and What Do They Believe In?* New York, NY: Cavendish Square, 2020.

Linsenmayer, Mark. *Philosophy for Teens: Core Concepts and Life's Biggest Questions Examined.* Oakland, CA: Rockridge Press, 2022.

Radford, Nick. *Philosophy for Beginners.* London, UK: Usborne Publishing, 2020.

WEBSITES

Crash Course Philosophy: Non-Human Animals
thecrashcourse.com/courses/non-human-animals-crash-course-philosophy-42/
Find out what philosophers like Peter Singer have to say about philosophy and animal rights.

The Hannah Arendt Center for Politics and Humanities
hac.bard.edu/about/hannaharendt/
The Hannah Arendt Center at Bard College provides information about the life and legacy of Hannah Arendt.

The Noam Chomsky Website
chomsky.info/
Noam Chomsky's official website contains an updated directory of his work and writings.

Peter Singer
www.petersinger.info/
Peter Singer's website provides links to his latest writing, podcast episodes, and related resources.

INDEX